HAUNTED PLACES

HAUNTED HOTELS

by Laura Stickney

BrightPoint Press

San Diego, CA

an imprint of ReferencePoint Press, Inc.
Printed in the United States

For more information, contact:
BrightPoint Press
PO Box 27779
San Diego, CA 92198
www.BrightPointPress.com

LIBRARY OF CONGRESS CATALOGING-IN-PUBLICATION DATA

Name: Stickney, Laura, author.
Title: Haunted hotels / by Laura Stickney.
Description: San Diego, CA: ReferencePoint Press, 2026 | Series: Haunted places | Audience: Grade 7 to 9 | Includes bibliographical references and index.
Identifiers: ISBN: 9781678211820 (hardcover) | ISBN: 9781678211837 (eBook)
The complete Library of Congress record is available at www.loc.gov.

CONTENTS

AT A GLANCE

- Many hotels around the world are considered haunted. Hotels are often historic buildings, and some were once used for different purposes, such as hospitals.
- Hotels are large places where many people come and go. Stories about people who visited or died there can make guests believe a hotel is haunted.
- Many people claim to have ghostly experiences during their hotel stays. They share firsthand accounts of these encounters. Common reports include hearing voices, seeing ghostly figures, or objects moving on their own.
- The Hotel Monteleone, 1886 Crescent Hotel and Spa, and the Emily Morgan Hotel are among the many hotels in the United States that people believe are haunted.

- The Stanley Hotel is famous for being the inspiration for author Stephen King's novel *The Shining*. A popular film based on the book came out in 1980.

- Ghost hunters often investigate supposedly haunted hotels. They use tools to try to detect paranormal activity. Some hotels have even been featured on ghost hunting TV shows.

- Many supposedly haunted hotels offer guided ghost tours or ghost hunting experiences. Guests can explore a hotel's most haunted rooms and learn about the spirits that are said to live there.

BLUE BATHWATER

Deborah McNabb was a sales manager. She worked at the Emily Morgan Hotel. This historic hotel is in San Antonio, Texas. McNabb had heard lots of stories about the Emily Morgan. Many guests said it was haunted.

The hotel was built in 1924. It had once been a medical facility. The seventh floor had housed **psychiatric** patients. And the basement was used as a morgue. That is

The Emily Morgan Hotel is one of several supposedly haunted locations in San Antonio, Texas.

where dead bodies are stored. Visitors often reported having strange experiences at the hotel.

One night, McNabb had her own unusual experience. She was staying overnight at the hotel. She and a coworker were rooming together. They left for dinner. When they returned, they were met with a strange sight.

In the bathroom, the bathtub was filled with water. But McNabb had not filled it. Neither had her roommate. "The bathwater had been run, and it was halfway full," McNabb said. "It was completely blue. . . . It was so blue that you would actually have to dye this water to be this color."[1]

McNabb and her roommate thought someone was pranking them. They decided

Some people think that things turning on and off by themselves, such as faucets or lights, could be a sign of a ghost.

to check the hotel's key card system. This would tell them whether someone else had entered the room. But no other key card had been used. McNabb believed the blue water was something **paranormal**.

HOTEL HAUNTINGS

The Emily Morgan Hotel is just one of many hotels that are considered haunted.

Flickering lights, unexplained footsteps, and moving objects are some of the many paranormal experiences people claim to have had at hotels.

Unexplained events have been reported at hotels around the world. Some guests report flickering lights and strange smells. Others have claimed to see objects moving on their own. Some people even say they have seen ghostly figures.

These chilling tales have made hotels popular with ghost hunters. They have also inspired many ghost stories. These grand buildings continue to capture the attention of curious visitors.

Many types of places are believed to be haunted, including hotels, houses, graveyards, and lighthouses.

WHY HOTELS?

People think hotels are haunted for many reasons. Sometimes it is because of a hotel's past. Many hotels have been open for a long time. The buildings may have been used for other things. The Emily Morgan, for example, was once a medical building. This means patients died there. Some people believe the spirits of the dead remain in the building. Something may be

Some hotels in the United States have been around for hundreds of years.

HOTEL

Humanlike and shadowy figures are common sightings at supposedly haunted locations.

keeping them from moving on after death. The spirits may cause paranormal activity.

The Emily Morgan's history seems creepy to some visitors. It may trigger people's imaginations. This may be why guests report strange experiences there. Some have spotted the ghost of a 1920s nurse.

She is said to walk down the hallways. Then she disappears.

Other guests notice unusual smells on the fourteenth floor. “That’s where they used to do surgeries, and so it smells sort of like [an] antiseptic type bandage smell up there,” said hotel general manager Kole Siefken. “Throughout all the renovations it’s gone through over the years, it still smells that way.”[2]

HISTORIC HOT SPOTS

Some hotels are considered haunted because of their history. Many hotels are connected to historical figures. Famous people may have stayed there. The Omni Parker House is in Boston, Massachusetts. It opened in 1855. Charles Dickens once stayed in a room on the third floor. Dickens was a famous British author. He was known for smoking cigars. Today, guests say they smell cigar smoke on the third floor.

The Congress Plaza Hotel is also known for its famous guests. The hotel is in Chicago, Illinois. Al Capone was a famous gangster. He reportedly used the hotel as a headquarters. Guests say his ghost roams the eighth floor.

Other times, a hotel's location makes people believe it is haunted. Some hotels are near historic sites. One example is the Hawthorne Hotel in Salem, Massachusetts. The Salem witch trials took place in the town. They happened from 1692 to 1693. The people of Salem accused others of practicing witchcraft. Twenty people were killed. The Hawthorne is near the site of this tragedy. Because of this, some people think the victims haunt the hotel.

TRAGIC TALES

Hotels are often large, grand buildings. They can have lots of rooms and hallways.

The Hawthorne Hotel is named after famous author Nathaniel Hawthorne, who was born in Salem, Massachusetts, in 1804.

Many people stay in hotels. Guests are constantly coming and going. Sometimes people die while staying at hotels. This is why they are often seen as hot spots for strange occurrences.

A hotel may be the site of a tragedy or crime. The tragedy may result in someone dying suddenly or mysteriously. Because of this, people may think the hotel is haunted.

Celebrity Ghosts

The Hollywood Roosevelt Hotel opened in 1927. It is in Los Angeles, California. Many celebrities have stayed at the hotel. These include actors Marilyn Monroe and Clark Gable. Several famous guests reportedly haunt the hotel. Monroe is said to haunt Suite 1200. She stayed in this room in the 1940s. People say Monroe appears in the room's mirror.

They believe something is keeping the victim's spirit inside the place where they died.

One example is at the Drake Hotel. The hotel opened in Chicago in 1920. Visitors say it is haunted by ghosts. One is the Lady in Black. In 1944, a woman murdered a hotel visitor. She was never caught. But people claim her ghost haunts the hotel.

The Lady in Red is also said to haunt the Drake. In 1920, she reportedly discovered her fiancé with another woman. So she decided to jump out of a tenth-floor window. Hotel visitors claim to have seen her ghost.

Stories such as these may make people see the Drake differently. The hotel's historic architecture can make it seem

The Drake Hotel sits along Lake Michigan in Chicago, Illinois. The hotel has ten floors and 535 rooms.

ghostly as well. Something strange might happen during a guest's stay. The Drake's environment might make people more willing to believe it is haunted.

Tok Thompson is a professor. He teaches at the University of Southern California. He said a place's environment can affect how people feel about hauntings. "If I asked my students in a classroom under neon lights how [many] people believe in ghosts, very few people will raise their hands," Thompson explained. "But, if we're all sitting together in some kind of **mausoleum** with gothic architecture in the moonlight and a wolf starts howling . . . then more people will raise their hands."[3]

Over time, people have shared ghost stories about hotels. Several hotels have developed reputations for being haunted. Whether or not these places are actually haunted, stories about them continue to fascinate people.

CHAPTER TWO

CHILLING ENCOUNTERS

There are lots of stories about haunted hotels. Some are stories from long ago. Others are more modern tales. Many hotel guests claim to have ghostly experiences during their stays. They share firsthand accounts of their encounters.

Several encounters have been reported at Omni Grove Park Inn. This hotel is in North Carolina. Some believe it is haunted by the Pink Lady. This is the ghost of a lady

Some supposedly haunted hotels are abandoned, meaning they are no longer used.

from the 1920s. She died after falling from a hotel balcony. She fell two stories.

Many guests have reported seeing the Pink Lady. She has been spotted in rooms and halls. Most guests say she appears as a pink mist or glow. Others have claimed to see the **apparition** of a woman wearing a pink gown.

People also say the Pink Lady moves objects in rooms. Sometimes she touches the feet of sleeping guests. One night, a mother and her son were sleeping at the inn. Suddenly, they woke up. They felt a cold stream of air in their room. But the windows were closed. Then they saw a pink glow coming from the bathroom. They had no idea where the glow came from.

The Pink Lady is believed to have stayed in Room 545 at the Omni Grove Park Inn. Some guests have reported unexplained events in that room.

GHOSTLY GUESTS

The Hotel Monteleone is another hot spot for ghost sightings. It is in New Orleans, Louisiana. Many guests think Maurice Begere haunts the hotel. He was a toddler in the 1890s. He and his parents often stayed at the Hotel Monteleone. Maurice died of a fever there.

After his death, his parents returned to the hotel every year. They visited on the anniversary of Maurice's death. They hoped to see their son's ghost. Maurice's mother claimed the ghost appeared one day. The encounter happened on the fourteenth floor.

The Thirteenth Floor

Many historic hotels do not label their thirteenth floors. They skip from the twelfth to the fourteenth. This is because of an old **superstition.** Many people believe the number thirteen is unlucky. It makes people feel anxious. In the early 1900s, hotel builders began skipping the thirteenth floor. The practice caught on. Today, many hotels still follow the tradition.

Maurice supposedly told his mom, "Mommy, don't cry. I'm fine."

Today, many guests believe Maurice still haunts the fourteenth floor. Some people have heard childlike laughter in the halls. Others think Maurice pranks guests in the hotel's elevator. They think he makes it stop unexpectedly at the fourteenth floor. This happened to a couple staying at the hotel.

One night, the couple was in the elevator. It opened on the fourteenth floor. As the couple walked through the hallway, they felt a chill in the air. They claimed to suddenly see the ghosts of several children playing. The ghosts were wearing old-fashioned clothing. They stared at the couple. Then they disappeared.

Ghost encounters have also been reported at Concord's Colonial Inn. This is one of the oldest hotels in the United States. It was built in 1716 in Concord, Massachusetts. It is near the site of the Battles of Lexington and Concord. These were the first battles of the American Revolutionary War (1775–1783).

The Battles of Lexington and Concord took place on April 19, 1775. Nearly 400 people were injured or killed.

During the war, the inn was used as a hospital for soldiers. Many patients died there. Room 24 was used as an operating room. Today, hotel guests report seeing the ghosts of nurses or wounded soldiers. Others say they have seen doors slamming on their own. Lights sometimes mysteriously turn on and off.

In 1966, Judith Fellenz was staying in Room 24. Fellenz woke up during the night. She had a strange encounter. Fellenz wrote to a hotel housekeeper about her experience. She wrote:

I saw a grayish figure at the side of my bed. . . . It was not a distinct person, but a shadowy mass in the shape of a standing figure. It remained still for a moment, then slowly floated to the foot of the bed, in front of the fireplace. After pausing a few seconds, the apparition slowly melted away.[4]

Since Fellenz's incident, other guests who stay in the room have reported similar sightings. Some have seen floating orbs or apparitions in the room. Others say they have heard unexplained whispering.

SPOOKY SIGHTINGS

The 1886 Crescent Hotel and Spa is said to house several ghosts. It is in Eureka Springs, Arkansas. Many people call it the most haunted hotel in the United States. From 1937 to 1940, the building was a hospital. It was founded by Norman Baker. He claimed to be a doctor who could cure cancer. Patients paid lots of money to stay

Certain rooms in supposedly haunted hotels might have more reports of paranormal activity than others.

at his hospital. But Baker was not actually a doctor. Many people died under his care.

Today, guests report seeing the ghosts of nurses and patients in the halls. And Baker's ghost has been seen in the lobby. Room 419 is reportedly haunted by a nurse named Theodora. People have spotted her outside the room's door. Some guests who

Some people believe portals in the Stanley Hotel allow spirits to move between the realms of the living and the dead.

stay in Room 419 say Theodora organizes their belongings. Others claim that she folds their clothes.

One couple who stayed in the room were curious about these stories. They purposely scattered coins around the room. When they came back from dinner, they claimed the coins were neatly stacked and sorted.

The Stanley Hotel is also known for ghostly encounters. It opened in 1909 in Estes Park, Colorado. The hotel has long been considered haunted. Guests report seeing shadowy figures throughout the building. Others hear music playing in the empty concert hall. Room 217 is considered the hotel's most haunted room. Elizabeth Wilson is said to haunt it.

In 1911, Wilson was head housekeeper. One night, she was lighting lanterns in the room. Suddenly, a gas leak caused an explosion. Wilson fell through the floor. She survived the fall. But many guests think her spirit remains in Room 217.

Unmarried couples who stay in the room say Wilson's spirit dislikes them. Some find their luggage packed by the door.

Other couples feel a cold force between them while sleeping in the room.

In 1974, author Stephen King stayed in Room 217. He and his wife were the only guests in the Stanley at the time. The hotel was closing for winter the next day. That night, King had a paranormal experience. He said:

> *I dreamed of my 3-year-old son running through the corridors, looking back over his shoulder, eyes wide, screaming. He was being chased by a fire hose. I woke up with a tremendous jerk, sweating all over, within an inch of falling out of bed.*[5]

The experience inspired King to write a book. It is called *The Shining*. It is about a writer named Jack Torrance. He, his wife, and their son move into a hotel as caretakers. Then strange things begin to happen. Jack descends into madness. The novel was made into a popular 1980 horror film. The story strengthened the Stanley's reputation as a haunted hotel.

Ghost stories can often make a place seem haunted even when there is no evidence of the paranormal.

GHOST HUNTING AT HOTELS

Many people try to investigate haunted hotels. These people are called ghost hunters or paranormal investigators. Some people ghost hunt as a hobby. Others are more serious. They use special electronic equipment. These tools are said to detect paranormal activity. However, most scientists believe these tools are inaccurate. There is no firm evidence of ghosts.

Ghost hunters travel around the world to investigate hotels that are thought to be haunted.

Nevertheless, many ghost hunters still search for evidence. Some even have popular TV shows. In each episode, ghost hunters visit a supposedly haunted place. Then they investigate it. They try to figure out whether it is really haunted.

In 2003, ghost hunters investigated the Hotel Monteleone. They were from

Ghost Hunting Technology

Ghost hunters use many tools during investigations. They may use night vision cameras. Some use voice recorders. One common tool is an electromagnetic field (EMF) meter. It measures changes in electromagnetic fields. These are spaces that contain electric and magnetic forces. Many people think EMF meters can detect the presence of spirits.

the International Society of Paranormal Research. The investigators stayed overnight at the hotel. They claimed to find several ghosts. Many were thought to be former hotel employees.

The group also investigated the hotel's restaurant door. Guests claimed to see the door open and close on its own. The investigators found that the door had a locking mechanism. To open it, a person had to push a button. This meant the door should not have been able to open on its own. The group claimed it discovered what was happening. It believed the spirits of a waiter and chef were responsible. The spirits were said to be fighting over whether the door should be open or closed.

TV INVESTIGATIONS

Hotels have been featured on many ghost hunting TV shows. One popular show is *Ghost Adventures*. Investigators use night vision cameras, recorders, and other tools to gather evidence. Then they decide whether they think places are haunted.

One 2011 episode focuses on the Cosmopolitan Hotel. This is in San Diego, California. In the episode, investigators stay overnight at the hotel. They see a strange light coming from behind a door. They hear unexplained banging. Their equipment also picks up ghostly voices.

Zak Bagans is one of the show's investigators. Before filming the episode, he spoke to a reporter. He said he wanted to investigate a bed at the hotel. A little girl died in it. Bagans said, "There's a lot of sadness; a lot of sorrow. There's even been claims of a woman who works downstairs who says she heard a little girl crying. I think it's . . . a **residual** energy that may be attached to this bed."[6]

The Cosmopolitan Hotel was originally built in the late 1820s as a home for a cattle rancher named Don Juan Bandini.

Sometimes, ghost hunters determine that hotels are not actually haunted. In 2007, the Hawthorne Hotel was featured on the show *Ghost Hunters*. Guests at this hotel would hear toilets flush on their own. Some heard weird noises. Others smelled the scent of apples in the hallways.

The *Ghost Hunters* team was able to explain many of these occurrences.

An electronic voice phenomena recorder, or EVP recorder, is a tool used to try to capture the voices of spirits.

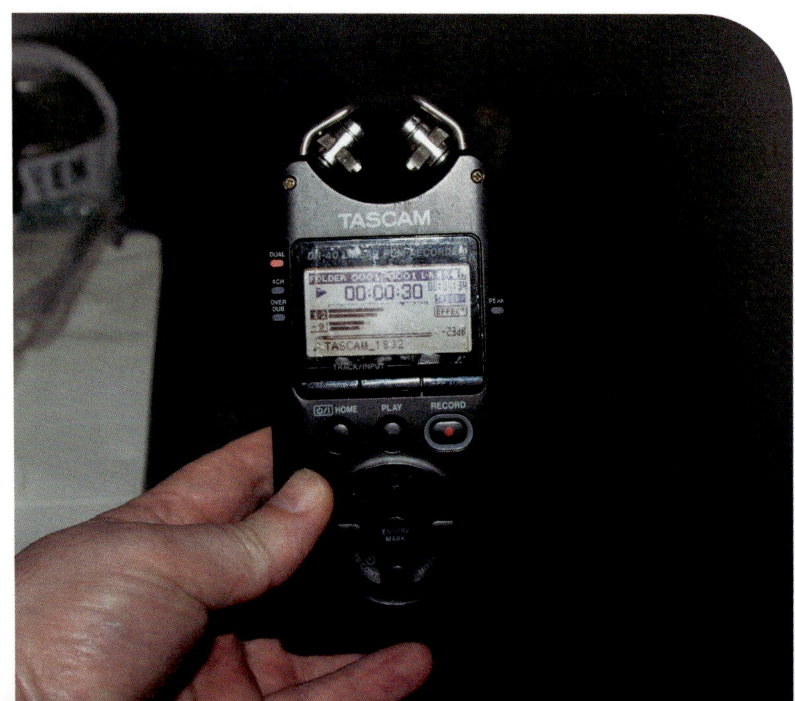

For example, the apple smell was coming from a janitor's closet. Old pipes in the wall were causing the noises. The team decided the hotel was not haunted.

CLUES AT THE CRESCENT

Many ghost hunters have investigated the Crescent Hotel and Spa. It has been featured on *Ghost Hunters*, *Ghost Adventures*, and other shows. In 2005, the *Ghost Hunters* team explored the hotel. In the episode, they set up equipment in several rooms. These included Room 419 and the morgue. The morgue is in the hotel's basement.

Several unexplained things happened during the team's stay. In Room 419, the investigators discovered their tools were moved around. In the morgue, they detected a ghostly figure on a **thermal** camera. The figure looked like a man in a military uniform.

In 2019, *Ghost Adventures* also investigated the Crescent. During its stay, the team claimed to contact a ghost called Michael. He was an Irishman who fell and died while building the hotel. Michael is said to be the site's most active ghost. He is known for playing pranks on guests.

After the crew finished filming, hotel staff discovered something. More than 400 glass bottles were found buried in the hotel's yard. Mike Evans is an archaeologist. He worked at the site. He said, "These bottles perfectly match with the posters and photographs of [Norman] Baker's bottles

Guests have reported unexplained experiences in several rooms at the 1886 Crescent Hotel and Spa, including rooms 218, 221, and 419.

at that time."[7] Baker would store tissue samples and tumors inside the bottles.

Today, ghost hunters continue to explore hotels. But other people can also go ghost hunting. Some hotels offer their own paranormal investigation opportunities. They invite curious guests to participate. Other hotels host spooky events. These experiences allow everyday people to be ghost hunters.

TOURS AND EXPERIENCES

Stories of hauntings often interest people. Because of this, many hotels embrace their reputation as haunted places. They advertise haunted rooms. Some offer guided ghost tours. Others allow local tour groups to visit. Some hotels also host special events for guests interested in the paranormal. They even set up spooky attractions.

Guides for ghost tours share the haunted history of a location with visitors.

Mercat Tours
Mercat Tours
Mercat Tours

Some cities have buses or trolleys that take tourists to different sites that are believed to be haunted.

The Crescent Hotel and Spa offers several ghost tours. Guests can pay to take a walking tour. Guides lead people around the hotel's most haunted rooms. The hotel offers a kid-friendly tour as well. People can also take part in the Crescent Midnight Investigation. This is a deeper dive into ghost hunting. It takes place at midnight. On this tour, people learn from paranormal investigators. They can try using real ghost hunting tools.

Many guests have reported ghostly experiences during the Crescent Hotel tour. One time, a tour group entered Room 419. A woman in the group had a camera. The camera supposedly took photos on its own. The woman later looked at the photos. Strange orbs of light were in them.

The Haunted *Queen Mary*

The RMS *Queen Mary* is in Long Beach, California. It was once a passenger ship. It was later made into a hotel. The ship is known for being haunted. Many guests claim to have seen ghosts on it. Today, visitors can take haunted tours on the ship. One tour allows guests to help with ghost hunting investigations.

On another tour, a man claimed to hear a ghostly voice. As the tour guide talked, the voice said the man's name. But no one else heard it. Another guest reported a paranormal experience in the morgue. During the tour, she felt someone's fingers on the back of her head. But when she turned around, no one was there.

La Fonda on the Plaza also offers ghost tours. This hotel is in Santa Fe, New Mexico. It is known for housing several ghosts. Guests can book the La Fonda Ghost Tour Package. The tour explores the hotel and other supposedly haunted locations nearby. Tourists have reported seeing the ghost of a man. He is said to be wearing a long coat. He has been reported in the hotel's lobby and hallways.

Guests on haunted tours often bring cameras in the hopes of capturing photos of ghosts.

WALKING TOURS

Some hotels work with tour organizations. Maryland's Lord Baltimore Hotel works with Poe's Magic Theater. This organization specializes in magic shows and entertainment. It regularly hosts ghost tours at the hotel. Each tour focuses on a different area. Featured areas include the ballroom and the lobby. One guest on the tour claimed to see a ghost in the hotel's ballroom. He glimpsed a man standing on the room's upper balcony. But when the guest looked again, the man was gone.

Other times, hotels are stops on local ghost tours. Williamsburg, Virginia, is

The Williamsburg Inn was built in 1937 by John D. Rockefeller Jr.

home to several haunted hotels. One is the Williamsburg Inn. Guests can sign up for the Haunted Williamsburg walking tour. Costumed guides lead guests around the area. They stop at haunted places, including hotels. Guests have reported strange experiences during the Williamsburg ghost tours. Several people have taken photos of historic houses at nighttime. Ghostly faces are said to appear in the windows.

The Hawthorne Hotel is also included in walking tours. Visitors can sign up for guided tours. They visit old buildings and graveyards throughout Salem. Many of these tours stop at the Hawthorne. A self-guided tour also includes the hotel. People have reported paranormal experiences during these tours.

OVERNIGHT EXPERIENCES

In addition to tours, many hotels offer overnight experiences. Guests can stay in a hotel's most haunted rooms. The Hotel del Coronado is one place that offers this experience. It is located in San Diego. Visitors can stay in Room 3327. In 1892, Kate Morgan checked into this room. She was later found dead on the hotel's staircase. People believe she haunts the hotel.

Those who stay in Room 3327 report strange experiences. Some claim to have seen Kate's initials appear on the ceiling. Others have felt someone touching their faces while they sleep.

The Stanley Hotel is known for its ghost experiences, too. Like other hotels, it offers

People who stay overnight in a haunted hotel may have a hard time sleeping because they feel uneasy or scared.

nightly ghost tours. But the Stanley also has tours focused on *The Shining*. Guests explore areas of the hotel related to the book and film. They can even see props from the movie. Hotel guests can attend spooky shows as well. These include psychic readings and **séances**.

In 2024, the Stanley also hosted a haunted weekend experience. It was called Overnightmare. Guests could stay in themed rooms. They could watch scary movies. They also enjoyed scare experiences. These involved actors, jump scares, and special effects. Guests could choose their level of scariness. Event planners said, "The thrilling experience starts immediately at check-in . . . and [continues] throughout the weekend with encounters of various characters and frights throughout the space."[8]

Many people are unsure whether hotels are really haunted. But they still visit in the hopes of experiencing something paranormal. Ghost hunters search for evidence of spirits. And reports of unexplained activity thrill people around the world. This is why haunted hotels continue to fascinate and frighten people.

FAMOUS HAUNTED HOTELS IN THE UNITED STATES

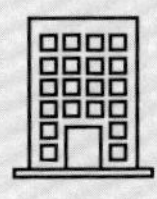

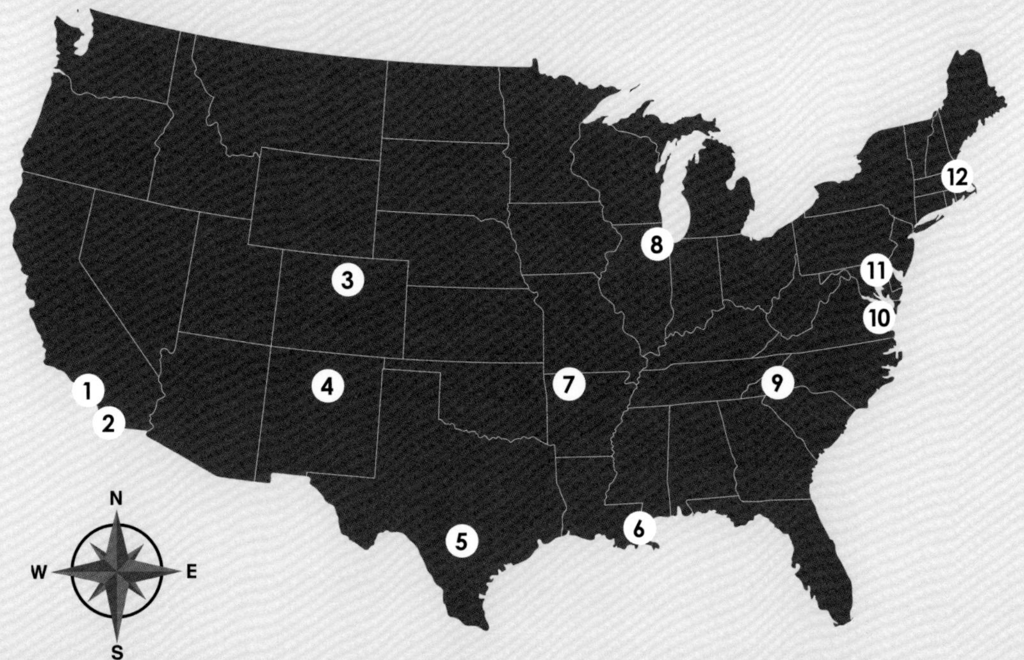

1. Hollywood Roosevelt Hotel: Los Angeles, California
2. Hotel del Coronado: San Diego, California
3. Stanley Hotel: Estes Park, Colorado
4. La Fonda on the Plaza: Santa Fe, New Mexico
5. Emily Morgan Hotel: San Antonio, Texas
6. Hotel Monteleone: New Orleans, Louisiana
7. 1886 Crescent Hotel and Spa: Eureka Springs, Arkansas
8. Congress Plaza Hotel: Chicago, Illinois
9. Omni Grove Park Inn: Asheville, North Carolina
10. Williamsburg Inn: Williamsburg, Virginia
11. Lord Baltimore Hotel: Baltimore, Maryland
12. Hawthorne Hotel: Salem Massachusetts

Many hotels across the United States are believed to be haunted. People visit these places to search for proof of ghosts.

GLOSSARY

apparition

a ghost or ghostly figure

mausoleum

a large, above-ground tomb

paranormal

something that is unexplained by science, such as ghosts or aliens

psychiatric

relating to the study and treatment of mental illness

residual

remaining after most of something is gone

séances

rituals where people try to connect with the dead

superstition

a belief that is not based on facts or reality

thermal

related to heat

SOURCE NOTES

INTRODUCTION: BLUE BATHWATER

1. Quoted in Brian Kirkpatrick, "Ghostly Nurses Outside Your Door. Tubs Fill Themselves with Blue Water. Gargoyles in Agony. Welcome, Your Room Is Empty," *Texas Public Radio*, October 29, 2021. www.tpr.org.

CHAPTER ONE: WHY HOTELS?

2. Quoted in Kirkpatrick, "Ghostly Nurses Outside Your Door. Tubs Fill Themselves with Blue Water. Gargoyles in Agony. Welcome, Your Room Is Empty."

3. Quoted in Hadley Mendelsohn, "Here's Why Ghost Stories Are So Important, According to a Professor of Anthropology," *House Beautiful*, August 23, 2022. www.housebeautiful.com.

CHAPTER TWO: CHILLING ENCOUNTERS

4. Quoted in "Concord, Massachusetts' Haunted Hotel," *1716 Concord's Colonial Inn*, n.d. www.concordscolonialinn.com.

5. Quoted in Monica Humphries, "I Stayed in a 112-Year-Old Hotel That's Been Nicknamed a 'Disneyland for Ghosts,' and the Stories I Heard Will Keep Me up at Night," *Business Insider*, October 15, 2021. www.businessinsider.com.

CHAPTER THREE: GHOST HUNTING AT HOTELS

6. Quoted in David Moye, "'Ghost Adventures' Crew Goes on Ghost Hunt of San Diego," *HuffPost*, July 21, 2011. www.huffpost.com.

7. Quoted in Bill Bowden, "Glass Bottles Found Behind 'Haunted' Arkansas Hotel Date to 1938 Cancer Elixir," *Arkansas Democrat Gazette*, April 12, 2019. www.arkansasonline.com.

CHAPTER FOUR: TOURS AND EXPERIENCES

8. Quoted in John Wenzel, "Stanley Hotel's Horror-Themed Weekend Drops Visitors into 'Insidious' and 'The Purge,'" *Denver Post*, September 25, 2024. www.denverpost.com.

FOR FURTHER RESEARCH

BOOKS

Carla Mooney, *Hauntings*. BrightPoint Press, 2025.

Richard Sebra, *Haunted Asylums & Hospitals*. BrightPoint Press, 2026.

Thomas Kingsley Troupe, *Haunted Hotels*. Crabtree Publishing Company, 2022.

INTERNET SOURCES

"America's Most Haunted Hotels and Inns," *US Ghost Adventures*, n.d. https://usghostadventures.com.

"Ghostly Happenings at the Crescent Hotel," *Crescent Hotel and Spa*, September 29, 2021. https://crescent-hotel.com.

"The Haunted History of the Emily Morgan Hotel," *Emily Morgan Hotel*, n.d. www.emilymorganhotel.com.

WEBSITES

Ghost City Tours

https://ghostcitytours.com

Ghost City Tours is one of the largest ghost tour companies in the United States. It offers hundreds of tours in different US cities. Haunted hotels are frequently featured on these tours.

Ghosts and Gravestones

www.ghostsandgravestones.com

Ghosts and Gravestones offers haunted tours and experiences in several US cities. Its website features information about ghost tours. It also provides facts about haunted places throughout the country, including hotels.

Historic Hotels of America

www.historichotels.org

Historic Hotels of America is an organization that shares information about historic hotels. It also creates an annual list of the top twenty-five most-haunted hotels in the country.

INDEX

IMAGE CREDITS

Cover: © A&J Fotos/iStockphoto
5: © Fabio Freitas e Silva/Shutterstock Images
7: © NeonLight/Shutterstock Images
9: © dtimiraos/iStockphoto
10: © Karolina_Marcinkowska/Shutterstock Images
11: © Zef Art/Shutterstock Images
13: © Anita Jambor/Shutterstock Images
14: © Dreamframer/Shutterstock Images
17: © Heidi Besen/Shutterstock Images
20: © 4kclips/Shutterstock Images
23: © Cristian Lipovan/Shutterstock Images
25: © Aleksandr Dyskin/Shutterstock Images
28: © Joseph Sohm/Shutterstock Images
31: © ChameleonsEye/Shutterstock Images
32: © Robert Kelsey/Shutterstock Images
35: © ThePalmer/iStockphoto
37: © Vink Fan/Shutterstock Images
41: © zhongyugan/Shutterstock Images
42: © Juiced Up Media/Shutterstock Images
45: © Patrick Horton/Shutterstock Images
47: © John P. Woods/Shutterstock Images
48: © chrisdorney/Shutterstock Images
51: © liebre/iStockphoto
52: © Anne Richard/Shutterstock Images
55: © Antonio_Diaz/iStockphoto
57 (hotels): © phipatbig/Shutterstock Images
57 (map): © Red Line Editorial

ABOUT THE AUTHOR

Laura Stickney is an editor, artist, and poet who lives in the Twin Cities area in Minnesota. She has never seen a ghost but enjoys learning about haunted places.